DELIA'S
CHRISTMAS
COMPANION

BBC

Contents

*W*hat I hope to set out here is a kind of chronology of all that the cook needs to do in the final 36 hours leading up to Christmas lunch. Even if you're not serving the traditional lunch set out below, you may still find it helpful to see some sort of framework into which different recipes can be inserted.

First, a word of caution. On paper a detailed plan of action can look quite simple and straightforward – but plans on paper can easily lull us into a false sense of security. It's all very well congratulating yourself on having the food organised, but have you allowed for those last-minute panics that only Christmas can create?

I have encountered more than my share of distractions – like not being able to find a Christmas tree on Christmas Eve (except the very scrawniest) and wasting half the day in the search. One year when we did buy one early it wasn't too steady in its tub and a visiting dog contrived to topple it over, scattering lights and cherubs, earth and pine needles to every corner of the room.

Don't forget, too, that people drop in unexpectedly at Christmas. That's one of the lovely things about it, and you just have to accept that you might be taking off your apron and pouring drinks just when you thought you had space to make the mince pies! So, given the inevitable disruptions, this countdown is not a rigid, don't-forget-to-set-the-alarm-and-put-the-cat-out list of orders. It's a few gentle reminders to help you through some busy hours.

◆●◆

The Christmas window at Charbonnel et Walker's shop in London.

✦ CHRISTMAS EVE EARLY AM ✦
Last-minute Shopping

In practice this means sallying forth for the freshest vegetables (sprouts, leeks, parsnips, onions, carrots, celery, swede, potatoes) and fruit (oranges, tangerines, grapes, bananas, dates, cranberries), because they need to last over the whole holiday. Everyone else will be doing the same, of course, so do get out early to join the queues and, before you leave the house, read your various shopping lists *out loud*. You may have forgotten something. Have you got any milk, cream, bread, pet food, the turkey . . . ?

✦ CHRISTMAS EVE MID-MORNING ✦
The Turkey Arrives

For my notes on frozen turkey see page 29, but let us assume your fresh and magnificent bird has reached its destination. There is no need to wash or wipe it, just place it on a sheet of greaseproof paper and remove the giblets. Make sure you know what it weighs: your supplier should have written it down – if not, you might find the bathroom scales helpful, but make sure you keep it on the greaseproof paper. Store it (uncovered) in the refrigerator till just before you go to bed. You may well need to remove one shelf from the refrigerator to house it, but if space is a desperate problem, don't worry: you can use an unheated bedroom, or the garage (with suitable covering) – even, in an emergency, the locked boot of the car which can be pretty cold on a winter's night.

GIBLET STOCK

However unpromising the giblets look, they make a wonderful stock for the turkey gravy and the meat from them will provide a splendid Christmas lunch for a deserving cat or dog.

The turkey giblets, including the neck and, if you're not using it for stuffing (see page 8), the liver

1 onion, sliced in half

1 carrot, sliced in half lengthways

A few parsley stalks

1 celery stalk (plus a few leaves)

1 bayleaf

6 whole black peppercorns

Salt

1½ pints (900 ml) water

First wash the giblets and put them in a saucepan with the halved onion, then cover with the water and bring up to simmering point. After removing any surface scum with a slotted spoon, add the remaining ingredients, half-cover the pan with a lid and simmer for 1½–2 hours. Then strain the stock and store, covered, in the refrigerator. I always think that it's when the giblet stock is simmering that you get the first fragrant aromas of Christmas lunch which fill you with the pleasure of anticipation!

→ CHRISTMAS EVE LATER AM →
Preparing Vegetables

A good time to get these chores out of the way. Always my choice for Christmas lunch are the tiny, tight *button sprouts* and I prefer to serve them plain as there are so many other rich flavours around. Prepare 1½–2 lb (700 g–1 kg) for 8–10 people, and keep them stored in a polythene bag in the refrigerator till needed. Another regular is parsnips: my recipe for these is *Parmesan-baked parsnips* (see page 20). They can be prepared in advance right up to the oven-ready stage. Store them laid out on a tray in the refrigerator or a cool place. Also at this stage take the sausage rolls out of the freezer to defrost.

→ CHRISTMAS EVE EARLY PM →
Make the Trifle and
Last-minute Christmas Mincemeat Cake

Christmas simply isn't Christmas without a trifle. I find this is the best time to assemble it. For the recipe see page 24. Also, if you've been too busy to bake your Christmas cake, it's not too late to prepare my wonderfully quick *Last-minute Christmas mincemeat cake* (see page 22).

→ CHRISTMAS EVE 3 PM →
Carols and Baking

The tradition in our house is to see to all the Christmas baking to the backdrop of the *Festival of Nine Lessons and Carols* on BBC television from King's College, Cambridge. In the past I used to bake my *Mince pies* and *Sausage rolls* (pages 19 and 27) fresh at this time of the day, but in latter years I have taken to cooking them from the freezer. For me this is the moment when Christmas really begins: I always enjoy joining in the carols as the lovely aroma of Christmas baking wafts through the house (even if I do get a bit grumpy because I don't like the old translation of the scriptures that are not always read very well!).

For baking the mince pies from frozen, and the sausage rolls, which should be well defrosted, the oven needs to be pre-heated to gas mark 7, 425°F (220°C). Return the mince pies to their patty tins, brush them with milk and bake for 25–30 minutes. Then remove them to a wire rack to cool before dusting them with icing sugar and serving or storing in an airtight tin. The sausage rolls should be arranged on a greased baking sheet, brushed with beaten egg and baked at the above temperature for 20 minutes, then cooled on a rack.

NOTE: In fact sausage rolls are really best eaten freshly baked, so if there is no immediate call for them, take them from the freezer and cook as necessary.

◆ CHRISTMAS EVE LATER PM ◆
The Turkey Stuffing

Now is the time to make up the stuffing ready to go into the turkey tomorrow. I firmly believe that the whole idea of stuffing a large bird like a turkey is to help to counteract the drying-out process during cooking. Minced pork (or pork sausagemeat) is an ideal ingredient for this because the fatty juices from the pork help to keep the flesh of the turkey moist. For this reason all the stuffings below have pork as a main ingredient. All the stuffings are for a 12–14 lb (5.5–6.5 kg) turkey.

NOTE: If you like your stuffing firm, so that it cuts in slices, add a beaten egg to bind it. If, like me, you prefer it crumbly, leave the egg out.

EIGHTEENTH-CENTURY CHESTNUT STUFFING

This recipe is adapted from one I first came across in the cookery book written by the eighteenth-century writer, Hannah Glasse. Peeling chestnuts (see page 29) is a chore at the best of times, but with the pressures of Christmas it can seem even more tiresome. So, if you can get hold of peeled chestnuts in a vacuum pack or container, that will make life infinitely easier.

1 lb (450 g) peeled chestnuts, cooked and very finely chopped
1 large onion, finely chopped
The liver from the turkey, chopped small
4 oz (100 g) smoked streaky bacon, finely chopped

1 oz (25 g) butter
4 tablespoons chopped parsley
1 dessertspoon chopped fresh thyme
1/4 teaspoon ground mace
8 oz (225 g) best quality pork sausagemeat, or finely minced pure pork
Salt and freshly milled black pepper

Melt the butter in a large frying-pan and cook the onion, bacon and chopped turkey liver for 10 minutes or so, until the onion looks transparent and everything is tinged gold at the edges. Now tip the contents of the pan into a large mixing bowl and add all the remaining ingredients. Season with salt and pepper, and mix very thoroughly.

TRADITIONAL PORK, SAGE AND ONION STUFFING

2 lb (1 kg) good quality pork sausagemeat or finely minced pure pork	1 heaped dessertspoon dried sage
4 heaped tablespoons white breadcrumbs	A little boiling water
1 large onion, grated or very finely chopped	1 egg, beaten (optional)
	Salt and freshly milled black pepper

American stuffing (see page 10).

Combine the breadcrumbs with the onion and sage in a large mixing bowl, then stir in a little boiling water and mix thoroughly. Next work the sausagemeat into this mixture and season with salt and pepper. Leave the stuffing covered in a cool place – but not in the refrigerator, as it shouldn't be too cold when you come to stuff the turkey.

AMERICAN TURKEY STUFFING

This type of stuffing was first served to me at a delightful Thanksgiving Dinner given by some American friends. The recipe, as many are, was handed down from grandmother to mother to daughter. This is my own adaptation, which keeps the variety of flavours and textures (see page 9).

6 oz (175 g) white bread, cut into ½ inch (1 cm) cubes

8 oz (225 g) onions, chopped fairly small

4 sticks celery, cut into ½ inch (1 cm) chunks

1 lb (450 g) best quality thin pork sausages, skinned and sliced into ½ inch (1 cm) chunks

8 oz (225 g) Bramley apples, cored and chopped

4 oz (110 g) walnuts, chopped

2 oz (50 g) butter

1 dessertspoon chopped fresh thyme

The grated zest of 1 small lemon

½ teaspoon ground mace

Salt and freshly milled black pepper

Begin by melting the butter in a large frying-pan and lightly fry the chopped onions, celery and chunks of sausage until they become golden at the edges (this will take about 10 minutes). After that tip these into a large mixing bowl and add all the remaining ingredients. Mix very thoroughly, seasoning well.

✦ CHRISTMAS EVE EARLY EVENING ✦
Accompaniments

In our family there are those who like bread sauce as the accompaniment to turkey, and there are those who prefer cranberries. For the latter I always make the following sauce, one of the very nicest and one that can be made ahead without coming to any harm.

CRANBERRY AND ORANGE RELISH

SERVES 8 PEOPLE

1 lb (450 g) fresh cranberries

The rind and juice of 1 large orange

A 1½ inch (4 cm) piece cinnamon stick

4 cloves

1 heaped teaspoon freshly grated root ginger or ½ teaspoon ground ginger

3 oz (75 g) caster sugar

2–3 tablespoons port

Chop the cranberries in a food processor, or else press them through the fine blade of a mincer, then place them in a saucepan. Now pare off the coloured part of the orange rind with a potato peeler and cut it into very fine shreds. Add these, with the juice of the orange, to the pan followed by the ginger, sugar and spices. Bring everything up to simmering point, stir well, put a lid on the pan and let it all simmer very gently for about 5 minutes. Then remove the pan from the heat, stir in the port and, when it has cooled, pour into a serving dish. Cover with cling film and keep in a cool place till needed. Don't forget to remove the cloves and cinnamon before serving!

Get Ahead!

If you're still on your feet by this time, you can also prepare the onion and cloves ready for the *Traditional bread sauce* (see page 14) and place in a saucepan covered with cling film. And why not weigh out the butter and sugar for the *Christmas rum sauce* (see page 15) and cover them in a saucepan ready for the off tomorrow?

⸻ CHRISTMAS EVE BEFORE YOU GO TO BED ⸻

In my younger days I used to dash off to Midnight Mass and return home with a group of friends for mulled wine, sausage rolls and pickled onions at about 1.30. Nowadays I like a good night's sleep before cooking the Christmas lunch, so I opt for an early night and morning Mass instead. Early or late, though, it is important to *take the turkey out of the fridge* now to allow it to come to room temperature so that it heats up immediately you put it in the oven. The same applies to the stuffing, and you also need to remove 6 oz (175 g) of butter to soften ready for the morning. Now your refrigerator will be looking on the empty side, so it's a good time to slip in the white wine, champagne, mineral water, children's drinks and anything else that needs to be chilled.

⸻ CHRISTMAS DAY EARLY AM ⸻
What Time is Lunch?

The specific timings that follow are those tested over the years in our house, but because lunch time will vary from one family to another you can adjust these timings to suit yourself. With young children you will doubtless be up early and want to eat lunch reasonably early; with older children it's not quite so important to open the presents at the first light of dawn!

For an average family-sized 14 lb (6.5 kg) turkey (oven-ready weight) I am calculating for a 2.00 pm lunch. If you plan to eat half an hour later or earlier, simply add or subtract 30 minutes to or from my timings.

Principles of Turkey Cooking

Many people have their own favourite way to cook turkey, usually because it's the way they were taught. I'm sure there is no best way, and I offer you the following method simply because it has always worked well for me and countless others. The turkey is placed in a 'tent' of foil, which essentially means it cooks in an oven within an oven. If you wrap the foil too closely to the turkey, though, it ends up steaming instead of roasting. Give it plenty of space between the flesh and the foil and it will roast in its own buttery juices without becoming dry. This method keeps all the juices intact. If you allow the bird to relax for 30–45 minutes before carving all the juices which have bubbled up to the surface will seep back and ensure the meat is moist and succulent (see opposite).

➤ CHRISTMAS DAY 7.45 AM ◄

Pre-heat the oven to gas mark 7, 425°F (220°C)

TRADITIONAL ROAST TURKEY

For a 14 lb (6.5 kg) turkey. See page 29 for timings for other weights of turkey.

1 × 14 lb (6.5 kg) turkey, oven-ready
6 oz (175 g) butter, softened
8 oz (225 g) very fat streaky bacon
Salt and freshly milled black pepper
1 quantity of stuffing (see page 8–10)

You will also need extra-wide turkey foil.

First stuff the turkey with your chosen stuffing. Loosen the skin with your hands and pack the stuffing into the neck end, pushing it up between the flesh and the skin towards the breast (not too tightly, because it will expand during the cooking). Press it in gently to make a nicely rounded end, then tuck the neck flap under the bird's back and secure with a small skewer. Don't expect to get all the stuffing in this end – put the rest into the body cavity.

NOTE: It is only dangerous to put turkey stuffing inside the body cavity if either the turkey or the stuffing is not defrosted properly, because the heat will not penetrate it quickly enough. If both are at room temperature it is perfectly safe.

Now arrange two large sheets of foil across your roasting tin, one widthways and the other lengthways (no need to butter them). Lay the turkey on its back in the centre then rub it generously all over with the butter, making sure the thigh bones are particularly well covered. Next season the bird all over with salt and pepper, and lay the bacon over the breast with the rashers overlapping each other.

Now wrap the turkey loosely in the foil: the parcel must be firmly sealed but roomy enough to provide an air space around most of the upper part of the bird. So bring one piece of foil up and fold both ends over to make a pleat along the length of the breastbone. Then bring the other piece up at both ends and crimp and fold to make a neat parcel.

Traditional roast turkey (see above).

→◆ CHRISTMAS DAY 8.15 AM ◆←

Place the turkey in the pre-heated oven, where it will cook at the initial high temperature for 40 minutes.

Once it is in, you can peel the potatoes ready for roasting and keep them covered with cold water in a saucepan. Now begin making the bread sauce.

TRADITIONAL BREAD SAUCE

SERVES 8 PEOPLE

4 oz freshly made white breadcrumbs (a 2-day-old white loaf with crusts removed will be hard enough to grate, but the best way is in a liquidiser, if you have one)
1 large onion
15–18 whole cloves or grated nutmeg
1 bayleaf
8 black peppercorns
1 pint (570 ml) creamy milk
2 oz (50 g) butter
2 tablespoons double cream
Salt and freshly milled black pepper

Cut the onion in half and stick the cloves in it (how many you use is a personal matter – I happen to like a pronounced flavour of cloves). If you don't like them at all, you can use some freshly grated nutmeg instead. Place the onion studded with cloves, plus the bayleaf and the peppercorns in a saucepan together with the milk. Add some salt, then bring everything up to boiling point. Take off the heat, cover the pan and leave in a warm place for the milk to infuse for 2 hours or more.

When you're ready to make the sauce (see page 15), remove the onion, bayleaf and peppercorns and keep them on one side. Stir the breadcrumbs into the milk and add 1 oz (25 g) of the butter. Leave the saucepan on a very low heat, stirring now and then, until the crumbs have swollen and thickened the sauce – approximately 15 minutes. Now replace the clove-studded onion and again leave the pan in a warm place till the sauce is needed. Just before serving, remove the onion and spices. Reheat gently, then beat in the remaining butter and the cream and taste to check the seasoning. Pour into a warm serving jug and stand until needed.

→◆ CHRISTMAS DAY 8.55 AM ◆←

Lower the oven temperature to gas mark 3, 325°F (170°C). *Now take a break!* At this point everything should be under control so you can take time out of the kitchen to help the kids unwrap their presents, have a coffee or tidy the house. After that prepare and set the lunch table, making sure you have all the right glasses for pre-lunch drinks as well as the table. It's a good idea to arrange the coffee tray now, too, and line up the brandy and liqueur glasses. Pop the plates and serving-dishes into the warming oven, and don't forget to warm a large plate for the turkey.

✦ CHRISTMAS DAY 11.30 AM ✦

If you're going to serve *bacon rolls* and/or *chipolatas* now is the time to prepare them, as follows: brush a shallow baking sheet with oil and arrange the sausages on it in two rows. For the bacon, stretch the rinded rashers out as far as you can, then roll them up very tightly, thread them on to long flat skewers and place them next to the chipolatas, ready to go into the oven later.

✦ CHRISTMAS DAY 11.45 AM ✦

Now is the time to finish off the *bread sauce*. Place it in a jug with some butter to melt over the surface, and keep it in a warm place.

✦ CHRISTMAS DAY 12.00 NOON ✦

Fill a saucepan quite full with boiling water, put it on the heat and, when it comes back to the boil, place a steamer on top of the pan and turn it down to a gentle simmer. Put the Christmas pudding in the steamer, cover and leave to steam away until 2.15 pm. You'll need to check the water from time to time and maybe top it up a bit.

✦ CHRISTMAS DAY 12.15 PM ✦

The Christmas pudding brings us, naturally enough, to the *rum sauce* whose time has now come. Make it as follows:

CHRISTMAS RUM SAUCE

SERVES 8 PEOPLE

3 oz (75 g) **butter**
2½ oz (60 g) **plain flour**
1 pint (570 ml) **creamy milk**
2 oz (50 g) **caster sugar**
3 (or more) tablespoons **dark rum**
1 tablespoon **double cream**

Place 2½ oz (60 g) of the butter in a saucepan with 2½ oz (60 g) flour, pour in the milk, then, using a balloon whisk, whisk everything vigorously together over a medium heat. As soon as it comes to simmering point and has thickened, turn the heat right down to its lowest setting, stir in the sugar and let the sauce cook for 10 minutes. After that add the rum, the remaining ½ oz (15 g) butter and 1 tablespoon cream. Pour the hot sauce into a jug, then cover the surface with clingfilm and keep warm until required.

✦ CHRISTMAS DAY 12.30 PM ✦

Increase the oven temperature to gas mark 6, 400°F (200°C). Now get some help, because you've got to get the turkey out of the oven and it's heavy! Remove the foil from the top and sides of the bird, and take off the bacon slices. Now baste the turkey very thoroughly with a long-handled spoon, then return it to the oven for a further 30–45 minutes to finish browning – give it as much basting as you can during this final cooking period. The bacon rashers can be placed on a heat-proof plate and put back in the oven to finish cooking till all the fat has melted and there are just very crisp bits left. (I like to serve these crunchy bits with the turkey as well as bacon rolls!)

✦ CHRISTMAS DAY 12.45 PM ✦

After you've dealt with the turkey, par-boil the potatoes for 10 minutes then drain them. Put the lid back on the saucepan, and shake the potatoes quite heftily in the saucepan so that they become fluffy round the edges. Now take a solid roasting tin, add 2 oz (50 g) lard to it, and place on direct heat to let the fat melt and begin to sizzle. When it is really hot, add the potatoes and (using an oven glove to protect your hands) tip the tin and baste the potatoes so all are coated with fat. Then place the roasting tin in the oven with the turkey.

✦ CHRISTMAS DAY 1.00 PM ✦

Now for the parsnips. Take another roasting tin and add 3 tablespoons of oil and 1 tablespoon of butter to it and place over direct heat. When the butter and oil are hot, add the parsnips and baste them in the same way as the potatoes. By now it will be time for the turkey to come out of the oven.

✦ CHRISTMAS DAY 1.15 PM ✦

Remove the turkey from the oven and increase the temperature to gas mark 8, 450°F (230°C). Place the parsnips on the middle shelf of the oven (with the potatoes on the top), and the chipolatas on the lowest shelf or floor of the oven.

Transfer the turkey to a warm serving plate: it will be fine left to relax in the kitchen temperature for up to 50 minutes loosely covered with double foil without losing its heat. Next pour the giblet stock into a pan and allow it to heat up gently. Tip the turkey fat from the foil into the tin, discard the foil, then spoon off all the excess fat from the roasting tin into a bowl. This fat is *precious*: it's wonderful for sautéeing potatoes, and have you ever tried turkey jelly and dripping spread on hot slices of toast and sprinkled with salt and pepper? A wonderful Boxing Day breakfast treat!

Mistletoe and seasonal plants, Berwick Street market, London.

Next make the giblet gravy. When you have spooned off the excess fat from the roasting tin and only the dark juices are left, work about 2 level tablespoons of flour into these juices over a low heat. Now, using a balloon whisk, whisk in the giblet stock, bit by bit, until you have a smooth gravy. Let it bubble and reduce a little to concentrate the flavour, and taste and season with salt and pepper. Then pour into a jug and keep warm.

CHRISTMAS DAY 1.30 PM

Turn the chipolatas and bacon rolls over, then you are free for a few minutes to go and have a pre-lunch glass of champagne. You deserve it.

CHRISTMAS DAY 1.45 PM

Pour boiling water over the sprouts, add salt and leave to boil for 5–6 minutes, then drain in a colander. While the sprouts are cooking, summon the carver and get all hands on deck to help dish up. And don't forget that lovely stuffing inside the turkey!

CHRISTMAS DAY 2.00 PM

Lunch is served. *Bon appetit!*

CHRISTMAS DAY (A LITTLE LATER)

Remove the pudding from the steamer and take off the wrapping. Slide a palette knife all round the pudding, then turn it out on to a warmed plate. Place a suitably sized sprig of holly on top. Now warm a ladleful of brandy over direct heat, and as soon as the brandy is hot ask someone to set light to it. Place the ladle, now gently flaming, on top of the pudding – but don't pour it over until you reach the table. When you do, pour it slowly over the pudding, sides and all, and watch it flame to the cheers of the assembled company! When both flames and cheers have died down, serve the pudding with rum sauce, or rum or brandy butter.

A very important message for all frazzled Christmas cooks. The good news is that what you now have, in addition to your aching limbs and heavy eyelids, is a house full of food and absolutely no more cooking to do. So stretch out, fill your glass and have a very Happy Christmas!

NOTE: all the recipes you need to complete the Christmas countdown can be found on the following pages.

TRADITIONAL MINCE PIES

·

MAKES 24

I will always cherish fond memories of my mother's and my grandmother's cooling trays piled high with freshly baked mince pies on Christmas Eve, ready to be packed into tins and brought out whenever friends popped in for Christmas drinks. The following is the traditional family recipe.

12 oz (350 g) plain flour	FOR THE TOP:
3 oz (75 g) lard	A little milk
3 oz (75 g) margarine or butter	Icing sugar
A pinch salt	
Cold water to mix	You'll need one (or two) trays of 2½ inch (6 cm) patty tins, one fluted 3 inch (7.5 cm) pastry cutter and one 2½ inch (6 cm) cutter.
1¼ lb (560 g) mincemeat	

PRE-HEAT THE OVEN TO GAS MARK 6, 400°F (200°C)

Make up the pastry by sifting the flour and salt into a mixing bowl and rubbing the fats into it until the mixture resembles fine crumbs. Then add just enough cold water to mix to a dough that leaves the bowl clean. Leave the pastry to rest in a polythene bag in the refrigerator for 20–30 minutes, then roll half of it out as thinly as possible and cut it into two dozen 3 inch (7.5 cm) rounds, gathering up the scraps and re-rolling. Then do the same with the other half of the pastry, this time using the 2½ inch (6 cm) cutter.

Now grease the patty tins lightly and line them with the larger rounds. Fill these with mincemeat to the level of the edges of the pastry. Dampen the edges of the smaller rounds of pastry with water and press them lightly into position to form lids, sealing the edges. Brush each one with milk and make three snips in the tops with a pair of scissors. Bake near the top of the oven for 25–30 minutes until light golden-brown. Cool on a wire tray and sprinkle with icing sugar. When cool, store in an airtight tin.

◆ ● ◆

Parmesan-Baked Parsnips

·

SERVES 8 PEOPLE

This is one of the nicest ways to serve parsnips, baked crisp and golden-brown in the oven with a Parmesan coating. They can be prepared well in advance, up to 24 hours, or they can even be prepared and frozen and will then cook perfectly if allowed to defrost first. This recipe also works very well with sweet potatoes.

2½ lb (1.25 kg) parsnips	Salt and freshly milled black pepper
6 oz (175 g) plain flour	Groundnut oil
2 oz (50 g) freshly grated Parmesan cheese	A knob of butter

PRE-HEAT THE OVEN TO GAS MARK 6, 400°F (200°C)

Begin by combining the flour, Parmesan cheese, salt and pepper in a mixing bowl. Peel the parsnips using a potato parer. Then halve and quarter them lengthways and cut each length in half across, so that you end up with smallish chunks. Cut out some of the tough woody centres. Now pop the parsnips in a saucepan, pour in enough boiling water just to cover them and add salt. Put on a lid, bring them to the boil and boil for 3 minutes. Meanwhile have a large kitchen tray ready. Then, as soon as they are ready, drain them in a colander and whilst they are still steaming drop a few at a time (with the aid of some kitchen tongs) into the flour and Parmesan mixture, shaking the bowl and moving them around so that they get a good even coating. As they are coated transfer them to the tray. Make sure you do them all fairly swiftly as the flour mixture will only coat them whilst they are still steamy! When they're all coated they are ready to cook or store in the refrigerator or freeze. Any leftover flour and Parmesan can be kept (sifted) in the fridge or freezer for another time. What is important is to have plenty in order to coat the parsnips quickly.

To bake them, place a large solid roasting tin in the oven to pre-heat and in it put enough groundnut oil just to cover the base and a knob of butter for flavour. Then, when the oven is ready, remove the tin and place it over direct heat (turned fairly low) and, again using tongs, place the parsnips quickly side by side in the tin. Tilt it and baste all the parsnips with hot fat, place the tin in the oven and bake them for 20 minutes, then turn them over, drain off any surplus fat (a bulb baster is good for this) and continue to bake for a further 15–20 minutes or until they are crisp and golden.

NOTE: If your roast potatoes are on the top shelf, these can cook beneath.

Parmesan-baked parsnips (see above).

LAST-MINUTE CHRISTMAS MINCEMEAT CAKE

This is a wonderful cake for the really harassed who meant either to make or buy a cake and never got round to it. It is unbelievably quick and easy yet has a marvellous flavour and a good moist texture.

1 lb (450 g) good quality mincemeat	The grated zest of 1 small lemon
8 oz (225 g) wholemeal flour	3 eggs, size 1 or 2
3 level teaspoons baking powder	4 oz (110 g) whole blanched almonds
5 oz (150 g) dark brown sugar	(only if you don't intend to ice the cake)
5 oz (150 g) softened butter or soft margarine	
6 oz (175 g) mixed dried fruit	You will need an 8 inch (20 cm) round cake
2 oz (50 g) walnuts, chopped	tin, greased, and the base and sides lined
The grated zest of 1 small orange	with greaseproof paper.

PRE-HEAT THE OVEN TO GAS MARK 3, 325°F(170°C)

First place all the ingredients (except the almonds) in a large mixing bowl. There is no need to beat the eggs, just break them in; but it is a good idea to sift the flour to give it an airing, then you can tip in the bits of bran left in the sieve afterwards.

Now, if you have an electric hand whisk, just switch on and beat everything together thoroughly. If not, a wooden spoon will do, but it takes a bit longer. Next, spoon the mixture evenly into the tin, level off the surface and, if you're using them, arrange the almonds in circles over the top.

Bake the cake for about 1 hour 30 minutes, or until the centre springs back when lightly touched. Then let it cool in the tin for 30 minutes before turning it out to finish cooling on a wire rack. If you want to and you have time you can 'feed' it with brandy, but it tastes wonderful anyway. When the cake has cooled, you may want to add the *Glacé fruit topping* (see page 23).

NOTE: It is important to use a good quality mincemeat if you are not making your own. In some of the cheaper brands there is too much liquid for this type of cake.

The cooking time for the cake varies from oven to oven, sometimes taking up to 2 hours. The only way to test it is to gently press the centre of the cake with your finger. If it is firm and springy, and no impression is left, then it is ready.

GLACÉ FRUIT TOPPING

·

FOR AN 8 INCH (20 CM) ROUND OR A 7 INCH (18 CM) SQUARE CAKE

A*t Christmas there are so many unusual glacé fruits available in the shops that seem to disappear at other times of the year. These can make very attractive alternative toppings for Christmas cakes. There are cherries (in all colours), glacé pineapples, peaches and I've even seen strawberries. You can, of course, use any combination you like. I've chosen dark glossy prunes to go with the russet colours of figs and apricots – there really couldn't be an easier or quicker way to top a cake. Just finish it off by tying it with a pretty Christmas ribbon. One point to note: the amounts of the fruits are approximate, since this will ultimately depend on how artistic you may or may not be.*

8 no-soak prunes	**1 heaped tablespoon apricot jam**
6 no-soak apricot halves	**2 tablespoons brandy**
2 no-soak figs, halved	
5 glacé cherries (or any other combination of glacé fruits)	

First of all, heat the jam and the brandy together in a pan, whisking well until they are thoroughly blended. Then, using a brush, coat the surface of the cake quite generously with the mixture.

Next arrange the fruits in rows or circles on top of the cake, making as pretty a pattern as you can. Brush the fruits, again quite generously, with a coating of the glaze. Then cool the cake and store in a sealed container till needed. The brandy acts as a preservative and the topping will keep well (stored in a cool place) for several weeks. Don't worry about the keeping-quality of this glaze – we have stored glazed cakes for three months and they were still in beautiful condition.

◆-◆-◆

CARAMELISED ORANGE TRIFLE

.

SERVES 8 TO 10 PEOPLE

I have been making the same Christmas trifle for years on end – but this year I decided to experiment with something new, without totally sacrificing the traditional qualities we'd grown to love. This fits the bill perfectly.

FOR THE TRIFLE BASE:

5 trifle sponges

2–3 tablespoons Seville orange marmalade

5 fl oz (150 ml) Sercial Madeira

2 bananas

FOR THE CUSTARD:

5 egg yolks, size 1

1 teaspoon cornflour

15 fl oz (425 ml) double cream

1 oz (25 g) caster sugar

A few drops pure vanilla extract

FOR THE CARAMEL ORANGES:

3 large Navel oranges

The grated zest of 1 of the oranges

1 tablespoon Cognac

1 tablespoon orange juice

2 tablespoons soft dark brown sugar

FOR THE TOPPING:

10 fl oz (275 ml) double cream, whipped

2 tablespoons hazelnuts, lightly toasted under the grill and roughly chopped

You will need a 3 pint (1.75 litre) glass bowl.

First of all split the sponges in half lengthways, spread each half with marmalade, then re-form them into sandwiches. Spread the top of each sandwich with marmalade, cut each one across into three, then arrange the pieces in the base of the glass bowl. Now make a few stabs in the sponges with a sharp knife and carefully pour the Madeira all over them, distributing it as evenly as you can – then leave on one side for the sponges to soak it all up.

Next grate the zest from one of the oranges and keep on one side. Place each orange on a board and, using your sharpest knife, pare off all the skin and pith. Then, holding each orange in one hand over a bowl to catch the juices – you will need 1 tablespoon for the caramel – cut out the segments by slicing the knife in at the line of pith which divides the segments (you need to cut each segment out with the pithy membrane left behind). Cut each segment in half and place in a small bowl together with the grated zest.

To make the caramel, dissolve the 2 tablespoons of soft brown sugar with 1 tablespoon of the reserved orange juice in a small pan over a gentle heat, and as soon as the crystals have dissolved turn the heat up to caramelise the mixture:

Caramelised orange trifle (see above).

it is ready when it turns one shade darker and looks syrupy and slightly thicker than before. Remove the pan from the heat and add the Cognac – this will make it splutter a bit, but that's OK. Pour the caramel mixture over the oranges.

Next make the custard. This you do by mixing the egg yolks, sugar, cornflour and vanilla extract in a basin, then in a saucepan bring the cream up to simmering point and pour it over the egg mixture. Whisk well, return the whole lot to the saucepan and re-heat gently, still whisking, until the custard has thickened (don't worry if it looks curdled at this stage: the addition of the cornflour will ensure that it will eventually become smooth once off the heat, if you work at it with the whisk).

Let the custard cool, and meanwhile strain the oranges, reserving the caramel juice. Arrange the oranges in amongst the sponge cakes in the trifle bowl, tipping it from side to side to make sure all the Madeira has soaked in. Now slice the bananas thinly and scatter these into the bowl, and push them down the sides as well. Next add the caramel juice to the custard and pour this on top of everything in the bowl. Cover with cling film and chill for several hours before topping the trifle with the whipped cream and scattering this with the toasted hazelnuts. Keep the trifle covered in the refrigerator and serve chilled.

SAUSAGE ROLLS

·

MAKES ABOUT 24

*M*ade with a melting quick flaky pastry, these are one of our major treats at Christmas. They can be prepared well in advance, frozen uncooked and then defrosted and baked from the freezer on Christmas Eve or whenever you need them.

FOR THE QUICK FLAKY PASTRY:		1 lb (450 g) good quality pork sausagemeat
8 oz (225 g) plain flour		1 teaspoon dried sage
6 oz (175 g) butter or block margarine		1 egg, beaten, to glaze
A pinch salt		
Cold water to mix		You will need 2 baking sheets, lightly greased.
FOR THE FILLING:		
1 medium onion, grated		

PRE-HEAT THE OVEN TO GAS MARK 7, 425°F(220°C)

The fat needs to be rock-hard from the refrigerator, so weigh out the required amount, wrap it in a piece of foil, then return it to the freezing compartment for 30–45 minutes. Meanwhile sift the flour and salt into a mixing bowl. When you take the fat out of the freezer, open it up and use some of the foil to hold the end with. Then dip the fat in the flour and grate it on a coarse grater placed in the bowl over the flour. Keep dipping the fat down into the flour to make it easier to grate.

At the end you will be left with a pile of grated fat in the middle of the flour, so take a palette knife and start to distribute it into the flour (don't use your hands), trying to coat all the pieces of fat with flour until the mixture is crumbly. Next add enough water to form a dough that leaves the bowl clean, using your hands to bring it all gently together. Put the dough into a polythene bag and chill it for 30 minutes in the refrigerator.

When you're ready to make the sausage rolls mix the sausagemeat, onion and sage together in a mixing bowl. Then roll out the pastry on a floured surface to form an oblong (as thin as you can). Cut this oblong into three strips and divide the sausagemeat also into three, making three long rolls the same length as the strips of pastry (if it's sticky sprinkle on some flour).

Place one roll of sausagemeat on to one strip of pastry. Brush the beaten egg along one edge, then fold the pastry over and seal it as carefully as possible. Lift the whole thing up and turn it so the sealed edge is underneath. Press lightly, and cut into individual rolls each about 2 inches (5 cm) long. Snip three V-shapes in the top of each roll with scissors and brush with beaten egg. Repeat all this with the other portions of meat and pastry.

If you are going to cook straightaway, place the rolls on baking sheets and bake high in the oven for 20–25 minutes. If you want to cook them later, store them uncooked in a freezer box and freeze until needed. Although you can store the cooked and cooled sausage rolls in an airtight tin, they do lose their crunchiness. For this reason I think it is preferable to remove a few at a time from the freezer and cook them as required.

◆ ● ◆

MULLED WINE

·

SERVES 12 PEOPLE

The following recipe has been donated by a friend. She says that the great thing about mulled wine is that you can keep adding to it. If unexpected guests arrive and you've no wine left, simply add some more water and fruit. Use the recipe below as a basic guideline, adjusting the quantities of wine if you want it stronger and adding more sugar or honey if you like it sweeter.

2 x 75 cl bottles medium to full-bodied red wine (Bulgarian Cabernet Sauvignon is ideal)	6 tablespoons granulated sugar or honey
2½ pints (1.5 litres) water	2 inch (5 cm) piece of cinnamon stick
1 orange stuck with cloves	2 teaspoons finely grated fresh root ginger or ground ginger
2 oranges, sliced	2 tablespoons fruit liqueur such as Cointreau, Grand Marnier or cherry brandy (optional)
2 lemons, sliced	

Put all the ingredients in a saucepan, then heat to simmering point, stirring until all the sugar has dissolved. Keep it barely at simmering point for at least 20 minutes – but do not boil or all the alcohol will evaporate. This can be made in advance, then re-heated just before the party. Serve it warm in ½-pint mugs (in which case there will be 12 servings) or else in 24 sturdy wine glasses.

◆ ● ◆

✦ TURKEY SIZES AND TIMINGS ✦

A good size of turkey for the average family is 12–14 lb (about 5.5–6.5 kg). This is oven-ready weight – which is equivalent to 14–16 lb (6.5–7.5 kg) New York dressed weight. But below you'll find cooking times for varying sizes of turkey.

It might be helpful to beginners if I give you an account of the exact timings of a recent turkey of mine. The turkey (14 lb/ 6.5 kg oven-ready weight) went into the oven, pre-heated to gas mark 7, 425°F (220°C), at 8.15 am. The heat was lowered to gas mark 3, 325°F (170°C), at 8.55. The foil came off and the heat was turned up to gas mark 6, 400°F (200°C), at 12.30. Then, with lots of basting, it was cooked by 1.15 and served by 2.00.

Cooking times for other sizes of turkey

8–10 lb turkey (3.5–4.5 kg):
30 minutes at the high temperature, then 2½–3 hours at the lower temperature, then a final 30 minutes (uncovered) at gas mark 6, 400°F (200°C).

15–20 lb turkey (6.75–9 kg):
45 minutes at the high temperature, then 4–5 hours at the lower temperature, then a final 30 minutes (uncovered) at gas mark 6, 400°F (200°C).

Please bear in mind that ovens, and turkeys themselves, vary and the only sure way of knowing if a bird is ready is by using the tests described in the recipe.

✦ FROZEN TURKEYS ✦

Try if possible to get a fresh bird. However, if you can only buy a frozen bird, or it's more convenient to do so, try to buy one that has been frozen without added water, then don't forget to allow plenty of time for it to de-frost slowly and *completely*. Always remove the giblets as soon as you can – with a fresh bird immediately you get home, with a frozen one as soon as it has thawed.

✦ NOTE ON PEELING CHESTNUTS ✦

Not a particularly easy job this, but the best method I have come across is as follows: rinse the chestnuts, then make a small incision in the flat side of the shell of each nut. Place them in a saucepan with cold water to cover, bring to the boil and boil gently for 10 minutes or so. Take the pan off the heat and use a draining spoon to remove the chestnuts from the water two or three at a time.

Peel these before removing the next batch. Take care to remove the inner skin from the crevices in the chestnuts.

✦ CONVERSION TABLES ✦

*A*ll these are approximate conversions, which have either been rounded up or down. In a few recipes it has been necessary to modify them very slightly. Never mix metric and imperial measures in one recipe, stick to one system or the other. All spoon measurements used throughout this book are level unless specified otherwise.

OVEN TEMPERATURES

Mark 1	275°F	140°C
2	300	150
3	325	170
4	350	180
5	375	190
6	400	200
7	425	220
8	450	230
9	475	240

MEASUREMENTS

1/8 inch	3 mm
1/4	5 mm
1/2	1 cm
3/4	2
1	2.5
1 1/4	3
1 1/2	4
1 3/4	4.5
2	5
2 1/2	6
3	7.5
3 1/2	9
4	10
5	13
5 1/4	13.5
6	15
6 1/2	16
7	18
7 1/2	19
8	20
9	23
9 1/2	24
10	25.5
11	28
12	30

WEIGHTS

1/2 oz	10 g
3/4	20
1	25
1 1/2	40
2	50
2 1/2	60
3	75
4	110
4 1/2	125
5	150
6	175
7	200
8	225
9	250
10	275
12	350
1 lb	450
1 1/2	700
2	900
3	1.35 kg

VOLUME

2 fl oz	55 ml
3	75
5 (1/4 pt)	150
1/2 pt	275
3/4	425
1	570
1 1/4	725
1 3/4	1 litre
2	1.2
2 1/2	1.5
4	2.25

Published by BBC Worldwide Limited,
Woodlands,
80 Wood Lane,
London W12 0TT

Further information and recipes can be found in *Delia Smith's Christmas*
from which this selection has been taken.

Delia Smith's Christmas
First published in hardback 1990
Published in paperback 1994
Reprinted 1994 (twice), 1995 (three times), 1996 (three times),
1998 (once)

ISBN 0 563 36048 8 (hardback)
ISBN 0 563 37064 5 (paperback)

Designed by Elaine Partington
Illustrations by Angela McAllister
Food photography by James Murphy
Location photography by David Steen
Front cover photograph by Norman Holland
Props by Andrea Lambton
Food prepared by Catherine Calland

This extract from *Delia Smith's Christmas* first published 1999
ISBN 0 563 55167 4 (booklet)

Promotional book exclusively available with *Delia's How to Cook*
Recommended retail price £3.99
Not for resale

Set in Baskerville by Keystroke, Wolverhampton
Printed and bound in Belgium by Proost NV, Turnhout.

Also available from Britain's most popular cookery writer:

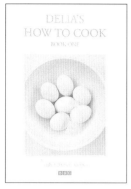

Delia's How to Cook: Book One
£16.99 r.r.p.

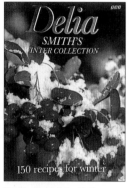

Delia Smith's Winter
Collection
£15.99 r.r.p.

Delia Smith's Summer
Collection
£14.99 r.r.p.

Delia Smith's
Christmas
£8.99 r.r.p.

Delia Smith's Complete
Cookery Course
£9.99 r.r.p.

On video:

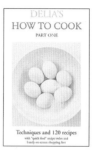

Delia's How to Cook:
Part One
£19.99 r.r.p.
(double cassette)

Delia Smith's Christmas
£12.99 r.r.p.

Delia Smith's
Winter Collection
£19.99 r.r.p.
(double cassette)

Delia Smith's
Summer Collection
£16.99 r.r.p.
(double cassette)

Published on December 9th 1999:

Delia's How to Cook: Book Two
£16.99 r.r.p.

Available from all good booksellers or
by order from the BBC Shop website
(www.bbcshop.com).
For mail order please call **0870 600 7080**.